They were an unlikely group. . . .

Under cover of darkness, Roe dropped the spy reports down a hole in one of Woodhull's farm fields. Once Woodhull uncovered the reports, he added his own intelligence. Then he looked through his spyglass for a signal from Anna's clothesline.

That's right—her clothesline!

When Anna stood on the bluff of Strong's Neck, she could see not only across the Long Island Sound, but also six different coves—three on either side of the point. Brewster gave each cove a number. Once she learned where Brewster was hiding, Anna returned to her clothesline. Then she used her laundry to signal Woodhull across the bay.

**The most exciting, most inspiring,
most unbelievable stories . . .
are the ones that really happened!**

GEORGE WASHINGTON'S SPIES

WILL CODES AND
SECRETS WIN THE
AMERICAN REVOLUTION?

by Claudia Friddell
illustrated by Wesley Lowe

A STEPPING STONE BOOK™

Random House 🏠 New York

The author and editor would like to thank Joseph Stoltz, PhD, Digital Scholarship Librarian, the Fred W. Smith National Library for the Study of George Washington, for his assistance in the preparation of this book. In addition, the author would like to thank Margo Arceri, Setauket historian and Strong's Neck resident, for her Tri-Spy Tour through the hidden trails of the Culper spies.

For my heroes, Rich and Coleen Davis
—C.F.

Text copyright © 2016 by Claudia Friddell
Interior illustrations copyright © 2016 by Wesley Lowe

Photograph credits: p. 90 Mount Vernon and p. 91 George Washington from the collection of the Library of Congress Prints and Photographs Division online at www.loc.org, p. 99 Benedict Arnold boot, some rights reserved by RDECOM

Visit us on the Web!
SteppingStonesBooks.com
randomhousekids.com

Educators and librarians, for a variety of teaching tools, visit us at
RHTeachersLibrarians.com

Library of Congress Cataloging-in-Publication Data
Names: Friddell, Claudia, author. | Lowe, Wesley, illustrator.
Title: George Washington's spies / by Claudia Friddell ; illustrated by Wesley Lowe.
Description: First edition. | New York : Random House, 2016. | Series: Totally true adventures | Audience: Age 7–10. Identifiers: LCCN 2016009900 (print) | LCCN 2016010628 (ebook) | ISBN 978-0-399-55077-5 (trade pbk.) | ISBN 978-0-399-55078-2 (library binding) | ISBN 978-0-399-55079-9 (ebook) | Subjects: LCSH: United States—History—Revolution, 1775–1783—Secret service—Juvenile literature. | Espionage—History—18th century—Juvenile literature. | Spies—History—18th century—Juvenile literature. Classification: LCC E279 .F75 2016 (print) | LCC E279 (ebook) | DDC 973.3/85—dc23

Printed in the United States of America
10 9 8 7 6 5 4 3 2 1

This book has been officially leveled by using the F&P Text Level Gradient™ Leveling System.

Random House Children's Books supports the First Amendment and celebrates the right to read.

CONTENTS

The Culper Spy Ring

Benjamin Tallmadge, alias John Bolton (agent 721), General Washington's chief intelligence officer and organizer of the Culper Spy Ring. A native of Setauket, he was Nathan Hale's best friend at Yale College.

Abraham Woodhull, alias Culper Sr. (agent 722), a Setauket farmer who lived with his aging parents and sister. Tallmadge chose him to lead the Culper spies.

Caleb Brewster (agent 725), an army officer under Tallmadge and the naval courier for the Culper Spy Ring.

Anna Smith Strong (most likely "lady" agent 355), wife of imprisoned Patriot judge Selah Strong. She assisted Setauket spies.

Austin Roe (agent 724), known as the Paul Revere of Long Island, who carried spy messages from Robert Townsend (Culper Jr.) in New York City to Abraham Woodhull (Culper Sr.) in Setauket. His cover was getting supplies for his tavern.

Robert Townsend, alias Culper Jr. (agent 723), New York City seaport merchant from Oyster Bay and the key Culper spy, who collected enemy secrets from British officers at James Rivington's coffeehouse.

A SPY IS BORN

On a chilly fall morning in 1753, twenty-one-year-old George Washington heads into the wilderness on his first mission as a soldier.

French troops are building forts in the Ohio River Valley. Major Washington has volunteered to deliver British orders for them to leave immediately.

But Washington isn't just a messenger. He's a spy.

Chapter 1
RIVALS

The Ohio River Valley was uncharted wilderness, but Washington was used to that. Before he became a soldier, Washington had been a surveyor, measuring land and making maps. He had slept under the stars, among wild animals, in all kinds of weather. He used the sun and a compass to find his way.

Washington's experiences living in the wilderness had prepared him for his difficult winter journey. But would he also make a good spy?

Lieutenant Governor Robert Dinwiddie of Virginia hoped so. Not only did he need Washington to deliver a royal order for French troops to leave the territory—he needed him to sneak back enemy secrets.

Washington had been a soldier for less than a year. He had no training as a secret agent. Could he outsmart the enemy?

As it turned out, he could.

Even though Washington was an enemy messenger, he was treated more like a friendly guest at Fort LeBoeuf. His charming personality fooled the French soldiers into spilling their secret plans for taking over the Ohio River Valley. Clever and confident, Washington drew detailed maps of the French forts and scouted sites for British forts without being noticed.

After a treacherous journey home, Washington arrived back in Williamsburg, Virginia, in January 1754. He handed Governor Dinwiddie the French commander's response to the British: the French weren't going anywhere. The governor wasn't happy, but he wasn't surprised. After all, the British and French had been rivals for years. Both countries wanted control of the Ohio River Valley.

Even though the French wouldn't budge, Washington's trip had been a great success. He had stolen important enemy secrets. The governor was wide-eyed when he read Washington's account of the journey. It was more like an adventure novel than a report! Washington had faced countless dangers. He had escaped Indian attacks. He had battled winter storms crossing the Allegheny Mountains—twice. He had even survived a trip down an icy river after getting knocked off a raft!

Governor Dinwiddie was so grateful for Washington's brave efforts, he gave him a promotion to lieutenant colonel. He also used Washington's journal to rally support for forcing the French out.

Dinwiddie had Washington's report printed

in the newspapers. British colonists from Massachusetts to Virginia read *The Journal of Major George Washington.* Even people in London were talking about the brave and clever young soldier from Virginia.

Two months after Washington's popular journal was published, he had new orders from the governor. He was to lead 150 colonial soldiers back to the Ohio River Valley to build and defend a British fort.

Soon after settling in a meadow near present-day Farmington, Pennsylvania, Washington, forty of his men, and twelve Indian comrades discovered soldiers hiding in a rocky glen nearby. No one knows which side fired first, but a skirmish began and within minutes, thirteen French soldiers were killed, including the French commander, Joseph Coulon de Jumonville. The conflict would later be called the Battle of Jumonville Glen.

Washington knew the French would send more troops. He also knew he didn't have enough soldiers or time to build a sturdy defense. Five weeks later, six hundred French soldiers surrounded Washington's men inside Fort Necessity, a frail shelter in the middle of an open field. For the first and only time in his life, Washington was forced to surrender.

• • •

In 1755, King George II decided that British troops—not colonial soldiers—were needed to force the French out of the Ohio River Valley. General Edward Braddock, the commander in chief of the British army in America, led 2,000 Redcoats to the Ohio River Valley. (British soldiers were nicknamed Redcoats because of their bright red uniforms.)

Washington wanted another chance to prove his worth to the British officers, so he volunteered as General Braddock's aide. On their journey west, Washington shared what he had learned on his earlier missions. The French and the Indians did not fight like the British. Although the Redcoats were some of the best-trained soldiers in the world, they were not prepared for frontier-style fighting. Washington also suggested that Braddock should gather secret intelligence about French battle plans—just as he had done.

Who knows what would have happened if General Braddock had listened to Washington's advice. Instead, the battle at Fort Duquesne was a disaster for the British. Braddock was killed along with over half the Redcoats.

Without hesitation, Washington took command of the remaining British troops. His fearlessness and quick thinking saved many lives. He managed to save his own as well—even after two horses were shot from beneath him and his hat was shot off his head!

At the age of twenty-three, Washington was promoted to commander of the Virginia militia. But even as the highest-ranking colonial officer, he ranked below every British officer. After three more years of loyal service in the French and Indian War, Washington still could not earn what he had dreamed of his entire life—a commission in the British army. He was tired of colonists being treated like second-rate citizens. So he turned in his uniform and settled into life as a farmer on his Mount Vernon plantation. George Washington was beginning to feel less like a British subject—and more like an American.

Chapter 2

START THE REVOLUTION!

Nine long years after Washington's first attack at Jumonville Glen, the British finally defeated the French in the French and Indian War. There was now a new king of England—King George III. King George insisted British troops were needed to protect the land they won in the war. He and the lawmakers in the British Parliament decided to keep Redcoats stationed in the colonies, even though most colonists didn't want them there. Those soldiers needed to be paid. But England was in debt after the long war. So where would all of that money come from?

The Parliament made a decision—since the

money was being spent in America, the colonists would have to pay!

And so, in 1765, the Stamp Act was passed. The colonists weren't given a choice—now they were charged an extra fee for everything printed on paper (even playing cards!) to help pay for the costly war and the remaining soldiers.

Taxation without representation, from a king clear across the ocean, made many colonists furious! Like Washington, more and more of them were beginning to think of themselves as Americans instead of British subjects.

Colonists who wanted to break away from British rule were called Patriots. A secret group of Patriots—the Sons of Liberty—organized protests against the British troops and tax collectors in America. They wanted to force the British to stop treating them unfairly. Some of the protests were violent.

Finally, the Stamp Act was dropped in 1766 after colonists refused to buy taxed goods. But that didn't stop the king. He decided to tax other things that the colonists needed, like paint, lead, glass, and tea. The protests continued until taxes on all goods were dropped—except for tea. The British kept the tax on the one thing the colonists would miss most every day. And that made many colonists mad enough to become Patriots!

Not all of the colonists were Patriots, however. Many thought it was wrong to turn against their mother country. They were loyal British subjects, after all. These Americans liked to be called Loyalists. Patriots called them Tories.

Since Patriots and Loyalists lived and worked together in the colonies, it was hard to tell them apart. Many Sons of Liberty members acted as spies. They found ways to revolt against the Loyalists and the British troops without anyone knowing who they were. The Loyalists had spies of their own. Some of them pretended to be Patriots and joined the Sons of Liberty to learn their secrets.

Patriot leaders urged colonists to stop buying British goods. Unfortunately, this didn't solve the bigger problem of being bullied by the British.

On April 19, 1775, British soldiers were sent to capture Sons of Liberty leaders John Hancock and Samuel Adams in Lexington, Massachusetts. The British also planned to capture Patriot ammunition in the nearby town of Concord.

When Paul Revere, a member of the Sons of Liberty, learned of the enemy's plan, he made a plan of his own. Revere had the sexton at the Old North Church in Boston hang two lanterns in the steeple. That signaled minutemen—Patriot volunteers—to get ready for a Redcoat attack from across the river. As clever and daring as any secret agent, Revere raced off to warn Hancock and Adams.

Revere arrived just in time. The Patriot leaders escaped and the ammunition was saved, but a British soldier fired his gun in Lexington the next morning. It became known as the "shot heard round the world" because it started the Revolutionary War.

Now that they were standing up to one of the best-trained militaries in the world, the colonies needed a united army. That was not going to be easy. Each of the thirteen colonies had its own

separate militia. The men were trained differently. They were made up of farmers and merchants, boys and old men, Southerners and Northerners. The new army needed a commander who could help them work together. They needed a leader with experience.

George Washington had not worn a uniform in over fifteen years. He was living a happy life with his new wife, Martha, and her children on his Mount Vernon plantation. And Washington was now a respected member of the Virginia House of Burgesses. His life in the military was over. *Or so he thought.*

Representatives from the thirteen colonies gathered together at the Second Continental Congress to choose a commander. They all agreed that George Washington was the best man to lead the Revolution. He had already proven himself as an extraordinary leader in the French and Indian War.

Washington did not think he was worthy of the job. But he felt it was his duty to serve his country. He agreed that it was time the Patriots banded together to stand up for their rights.

Could the Virginia farmer take command of the Continental army? He would have to find a way to lead a motley group of untrained volunteers into battle against one of the most disciplined armies in the world.

There was no time to waste. The war had already begun. Washington dusted off his uniform and packed up his military experience.

Including his skills as a spy.

Chapter 3

WASHINGTON NEEDS
A SPY RING

General George Washington arrived in Boston in July 1775 to take command of the Continental troops. Without enough ammunition, food, and supplies for his men, he remained patient throughout the fall and winter. Finally, in March 1776—using secret plans and captured cannons—the Patriots were able to drive the British from Boston.

Now that Boston was back in Patriot control, Washington needed to focus on an even more important location: New York.

New York Harbor was the gateway for goods, communication, and transportation between the

northern and southern colonies. If the British could control the busy waterways of New York, it would put them in a good position to win the war.

Thousands of British troops poured into New York Harbor. Royal Navy ships crowded the seaport. Washington knew he didn't have enough troops or ammunition to defeat the British if they attacked. The Patriots needed inside knowledge of enemy plans.

As it turned out, New York Harbor was also the perfect gateway for spies.

• • •

General Washington desperately needed his own secret agents. But whom could he trust? Traitors seemed to be lurking everywhere.

During the summer of 1775, Dr. Benjamin Church—the chief physician of the Continental army and a Sons of Liberty member—was caught sneaking secrets to the British. Washington was shocked. Patriots later discovered that the British attack on Lexington and Concord was accomplished thanks to Dr. Church's stolen secrets.

The following summer, Thomas Hickey, one of General Washington's personal bodyguards, was arrested in New York for using counterfeit money. While Hickey sat in jail, he admitted to a much worse crime. Hickey told a fellow prisoner that he was also part of a secret plot to kidnap and kill General Washington!

Washington made it clear he had no tolerance for traitors. Dr. Church was exiled, and Hickey was the first person to be executed for treason against America.

Washington needed his own dependable spies. But most soldiers at that time did not consider spying an honorable way to serve one's country. There was nothing heroic about sneaking around and lying in order to steal enemy information—was there?

A young Patriot named Nathan Hale thought there was.

• • •

In the fall of 1776, Washington's Continental army suffered many defeats. The British were taking control of New York one battle at a time.

The Americans were losing ground quickly. Washington needed someone to cross into Long Island—now controlled by the British—to gather enemy intelligence. He was desperate for news about Redcoat supplies, troop movements, and future attacks.

Nathan Hale, a twenty-one-year-old captain in the 19th Connecticut Regiment, wanted to help. A year earlier, Hale had received a letter from his college friend Benjamin Tallmadge that inspired him to join the fight for independence. Eager to serve, Hale volunteered to spy for General Washington.

Under instruction from Washington, Hale set out for Long Island. He pretended to be a teacher looking for work. It seemed to be the perfect cover for moving around alone in enemy territory. After all, Hale had been an actor at Yale and a teacher before joining the army.

Unfortunately, his act was not convincing enough. Major Robert Rogers, a British hero from the French and Indian War, outsmarted the young Patriot and captured him. Hale's first mission would be his last. After confessing to being an enemy spy, Hale was hanged by his British captors.

The news of Hale's death greatly distressed Washington. Why had he sent someone so inexperienced on such a dangerous mission all alone? Washington felt he was responsible for Hale's tragic fate. He would not make the same mistake again.

Washington was now convinced that a group of spies—not a solo agent—had a better chance of outsmarting the British in New York. He needed a spymaster—someone he trusted to find exactly the right group of people to handle the dangerous missions back and forth between Long Island and Manhattan. He needed someone who could oversee the spies and deliver enemy secrets to him in Patriot territory.

As it turned out, Hale's closest college friend was just the man for the job.

Chapter 4

SPYMASTER

Benjamin Tallmadge—unlike his ill-fated friend Nathan Hale—saw a lot of action on the battlefields. He moved up the ranks in the Continental Army quickly. Through loyal service and brave leadership, Tallmadge soon became one of General Washington's most trusted officers.

Tallmadge did not come from a military family. He had started out on a more scholarly path. Tutored by his preacher father in Setauket, Long Island, young Benjamin was accepted into Yale College at the age of twelve. Too young for college life, he stayed home until he was fifteen.

Well prepared and bright beyond his years,

Tallmadge was often bored by his studies during his first two years of college. He preferred more entertaining activities outside the classroom, such as debating and acting in theater productions with Hale.

After graduating in 1773, both Tallmadge and Hale settled into teaching positions at Connecticut schools. Tallmadge had planned to go to law school, but his patriotism was sparked when he traveled to Boston to see the turmoil of revolution

for himself. Once he knew there was little hope for peace with Britain, Tallmadge was eager to serve his new country.

• • •

Lieutenant Tallmadge proved to be a brave and clever soldier. General Washington gained great respect for him during the brutal winter months at Valley Forge.

In November 1778, George Washington promoted Major Tallmadge to director of military intelligence. His new job was to organize a spy ring in New York to keep Washington informed about enemy supplies and troop movements.

Major Tallmadge had his own reasons for wanting to take on such a risky job. The same month his friend Hale was captured and killed, the British had also arrested Tallmadge's oldest brother, William. After learning that William had died from starvation and neglect on a British prison ship, Tallmadge was determined to get the information Washington needed to defeat the British.

Unlike Hale, who had never been to Long Island before his failed spy mission, Tallmadge had grown up there, traveling the roads, the forests, and the waterways. He knew the people, their customs, and their habits.

It was Tallmadge's job to find someone from Long Island he could trust to organize and manage the spies. He needed someone who knew the countryside—someone who had a reason to regularly cross the East River from Long Island into New York City. Most important, he needed someone who *didn't* stand out as a Patriot.

Tallmadge had an idea that Abraham Woodhull, his childhood friend from Setauket, would make the perfect spy.

Chapter 5

SETAUKET SPIES

Abraham Woodhull seemed an unlikely spy to everyone except Major Tallmadge. He was a farmer who had had little schooling. When both his brothers died, Woodhull was left with the responsibility of farming the family fields and caring for his sister and aging parents.

Woodhull had never shown strong feelings about the war one way or the other. He had served only two months in the New York militia in 1775. But his feelings changed when his older cousin Brigadier General Nathaniel Woodhull was captured after the Battle of Long Island. General Woodhull had been a wise and respected officer.

After hearing about his cousin's death from the Redcoats' cruel treatment, Abraham Woodhull quietly seethed with anger.

Tallmadge guessed that Woodhull hated the British for what they had done to his cousin. He also knew that his childhood friend was in a Patriot jail for smuggling farm produce across Long Island Sound to sell to the British. Hating them didn't prevent Woodhull from trading for their silver!

Tallmadge wondered if he could talk his old friend into serving his country without putting on a uniform or picking up a weapon. So he offered Woodhull a deal that would get him out of jail. It would involve smuggling cargo much more dangerous than vegetables.

Woodhull agreed to lead Tallmadge's spy ring in the fall of 1778. The first order of business was for Woodhull to publicly pledge his allegiance to the Crown in the town square. Tallmadge thought this would help to prove Woodhull was a devoted Loyalist.

Next, Tallmadge needed to create secret code names for his Setauket spies. Washington had already given the spy ring the code name Culper. It was a nod to Culpeper, Virginia—the county he surveyed when he was seventeen.

Tallmadge gave himself the code name John Bolton. That was ordinary enough. Then he gave Woodhull the code name Samuel Culper. Samuel was Tallmadge's brother's name. The last name Culper signaled that Woodhull was the leader of the spy ring.

Woodhull began making regular trips to Manhattan to gather intelligence. But he didn't always have vegetables to sell. So why else would a farmer need to take frequent trips into enemy territory?

Fortunately, Abraham Woodhull had a sister, Mary, who lived in New York City. She and her husband, Amos Underhill, had recently opened a boardinghouse near Manhattan's seaport. In addition to selling his produce, Woodhull's visits to his sister gave him another reason to travel to the center of British naval activity.

But Woodhull's 110-mile trips back and forth between Setauket and New York City were dangerous. And that was only half the journey. Woodhull then needed someone to smuggle his secrets by boat from Setauket across Long Island Sound to Tallmadge, who was stationed in Connecticut. Tallmadge and Woodhull agreed there was only one man for the job—their childhood friend Caleb Brewster.

Like Woodhull, Brewster preferred the outdoors to the classroom. But his dreams of adventure reached far beyond the farm fields and forests of Long Island. When he was nineteen, Brewster joined a whaleboat crew headed for

Greenland. He then sailed on a merchant ship to London.

When Brewster returned to America, the Revolutionary War was under way. He immediately joined the freedom fighters. Brewster was now an experienced seaman. He was also a daredevil.

Brewster piloted small whaleboats in the enemy-controlled waters of Long Island Sound. He and his bold crew rowed across the Devil's Belt in the dark of the night to attack and rob British supply ships. Brewster saw enemy ship movements firsthand. He had already sent British naval intelligence directly to Washington, earning the general's trust.

Tallmadge and Woodhull knew they could trust Brewster. Their families had been neighbors for generations. Once Brewster was invited to join the Setauket spy ring, he needed no convincing.

He was ready and eager to smuggle Culper secrets.

Boisterous and bold, Brewster made no secret of being a Patriot spy. The British knew he was sneaking intelligence back and forth across the Devil's Belt. They just couldn't catch him!

Now that Woodhull was supposed to be a Loyalist, he avoided being seen with Brewster. Their meetings might look suspicious to the British troops who had taken over their hometown. And if one spy was discovered, it could endanger the others.

So how could they transfer their messages without being caught? Woodhull invited another family friend and neighbor to signal their secret meetings. It would take a brave and clever spy to outsmart the Redcoats right in front of their eyes.

● ● ●

Anna Smith Strong was ten years older than the other Setauket spies, but she and her husband, Selah, had known them all their lives. Their families had been neighbors for generations.

Anna may have found her reason for helping

the Culper spies when Selah, a Patriot judge, was arrested for "surreptitious correspondence with the enemy." That meant the British thought he was a spy!

Selah was taken from his family and sent to a British prison. Anna, a brave and devoted wife, was determined to free her husband. It helped that she had important Tory relatives in New York. She was allowed to take meals to her husband so he would not starve.

While Selah was in prison, British troops moved into the Strongs' manor house at Strong's Neck. The house was one of the grand estates on the North Shore of Long Island. The point on Strong's Neck overlooked Long Island Sound across to Connecticut. It was the perfect location for a British base.

Eventually, a relative of Anna's helped free Selah. But it was too dangerous for him to return to Setauket, so he moved to Patriot territory in Connecticut. Someone needed to remain in Setauket to watch after the family estate. As dangerous as it was to stay, Anna would not desert her family's home—even if it meant sharing it with the enemy.

When British soldiers moved into her house, Anna moved to a small cottage on the estate. From her clothesline, she could see Woodhull's farm across a small bay. It was the ideal spot for sending signals.

• • •

Travel between Setauket and New York City became more and more dangerous. Travelers— Patriots and Tories alike—never knew when they might be searched, robbed, or even attacked. Redcoats and Loyalist highwaymen were known to be ruthless. There were no rules when it came to traveling in enemy territory.

Woodhull worried constantly about getting

caught. After a few close calls at checkpoints, he decided he needed another messenger to share the long and nerve-racking trips to and from New York City.

So he turned to other childhood friends.

Jonas Hawkins, a Setauket friend and neighbor, was the first courier who brought messages from New York to Setauket. But Jonas became nervous after nearly getting caught. Luckily, Austin Roe was willing to take his place in the risky business of transporting spy secrets. Roe had also grown up with the other Setauket spies. He had recently bought a house from the Woodhull family and opened Roe Tavern. Besides offering food and drink there, he had rooms for overnight guests. Now he needed to make frequent trips to New York City to buy food and other supplies for his busy inn.

Roe had the perfect reason for traveling between Setauket and the seaport. He could bring back secrets hidden inside his deliveries. What a relief it was for Woodhull when Roe agreed to be a courier for the spy ring!

Woodhull knew he could trust his Setauket friends with revolutionary secrets. Now it was time to find dependable spies across the East River—in New York City.

Chapter 6

THE NEW YORK CULPERS

Woodhull knew that his ability to gather enemy secrets was limited. He couldn't wander around the New York City seaport all day when he was supposed to be visiting his sister. And he couldn't visit his sister often when he was supposed to be busy in Setauket, taking care of his family and farm. Woodhull was worried that he looked suspicious. As it turned out, he had good reason.

On the night of June 5, 1779, Colonel John Graves Simcoe, commander of a British regiment called the Queen's Rangers, got a tip: the quiet farmer Abraham Woodhull just might be gathering British secrets on his frequent trips to New York City.

Ordering his men to surround Woodhull's home, Simcoe forced his way in and searched for the Patriot spy. But Woodhull wasn't there. Simcoe was furious and took his anger out on Abraham's father instead.

When Abraham returned home, he found his father beaten and his family terrified. Only luck had saved him from being captured or killed by Simcoe that night. Now Woodhull was more than worried. It was time to find someone else who could gather enemy secrets in New York.

In the fall of 1778, Colonel Simcoe and 300 of his Queen's Rangers had settled in for the winter in Oyster Bay, a town on the North Shore of Long Island about thirty-five miles away from Setauket. The colonel chose Samuel Townsend's home as his headquarters for the winter months.

A Quaker, Samuel Townsend did not believe in violence or war. Quakers tended to be Loyalists. It was against their beliefs to fight or revolt against government. Yet Samuel had been outspoken for a Quaker. He got himself into trouble after complaining about the British. The Redcoats kept him quiet by making him take an oath of allegiance to the Crown. Now they were living in his house.

Robert Townsend, Samuel's son, owned a dry-goods store with his brother and cousin in New York City's seaport. Private and shy, Robert acted more like a Quaker than his father.

Months after Simcoe and his Rangers moved into the Townsend home, Robert came to Oyster Bay for a visit. He could not believe his eyes. The British soldiers had destroyed their lovely village. They had chopped down every tree in his father's prized apple orchard for wood. They bullied his family and their friends. Even their Loyalist neighbors weren't safe from the cruel British intruders.

Robert returned to his job across the East River a changed man. He had to do something to help his family and his town. But he wasn't a soldier. He was a peaceful Quaker and a businessman. How could *he* fight the British?

Townsend found his answer at the Underhills' boardinghouse. While he was a boarder there, he got to know Mary Underhill's brother, Abraham Woodhull. In the summer of 1779, Woodhull convinced Townsend that he could, in his own way, help fight the British. After all, Townsend overheard British commanders and Loyalists talk while they shopped in his store. He had good reason to observe ship and troop movements when he checked on his own shipments at the docks. Townsend had the perfect cover for a spy!

Woodhull gave Townsend the code name Culper Jr. He then changed his own code name to Culper Sr. Townsend insisted that only Woodhull and Roe, the courier who delivered the messages, know his name. Not even General Washington could ever know his true identity.

The general was pleased to have a spy based right in the middle of New York's seaport. Washington sent a detailed list of instructions to his Culper spies and agreed that Culper Jr.'s identity should remain secret, even from him.

It didn't take long for Townsend to prove himself a reliable and resourceful spy. Just as Woodhull had thought, Culper Jr. was in an excellent position to gather important enemy news.

Washington instructed his spies to "mix as much as possible among the Officers and Refugees [Tories], visit the Coffee Houses and all public places." Townsend soon realized he could do even more to earn the trust of the British.

Just a few blocks away from Townsend's shop was James Rivington's print shop and coffeehouse. Rivington was an outspoken Loyalist. His newspaper, the *Royal Gazette,* was a Tory paper that openly supported King George and boldly attacked all things American.

Before the British had taken control of New York, a Sons of Liberty gang had broken into Rivington's shop and destroyed his printing press. Rivington had to move his family back to England to get out of harm's way. But in 1777, once the British were in control of New York, he returned to the seaport with a new press and was back in business.

Townsend had an idea that would give him cover to gather even more enemy secrets. He volunteered to write a column for Rivington's newspaper, reporting local news.

What a clever plan! Now Culper Jr. was a reporter for the most popular Loyalist newspaper. He was *expected* to ask Loyalists and British soldiers about their business. It was natural for Townsend to rub elbows with British officers at Rivington's coffeehouse. Who would suspect a Tory journalist as a spy?

Chapter 7

SECRET CODES AND
DANGEROUS TRAILS

It was Woodhull's job to direct the Culper spies, but it was up to Tallmadge to devise a plan for keeping the messages secret. There was no spy-training book for Tallmadge to read. There was no codebook for him to study. He had to depend on his own ideas, General Washington's advice, and his spies' good judgment to safely transport enemy secrets.

Tallmadge needed a way to disguise enemy news. He decided to write his own codebook, which he called the numerical dictionary because it traded numbers for words. For example, each spy had his own special number. Tallmadge was 721, and Robert Townsend was 723. Even Washington had a code number, 711. Ordinary words were coded by number as well. For example, 48.87 was code for *be careful!*

For words that were not found in his codebook, Tallmadge used a secret code that traded letters for other letters. Here was his cipher code for letters:

a	b	c	d	e	f	g	h	i	j	k	l	m	n	o	p	q	r	s	t	u	v	w	x	y
e	f	g	h	i	j	a	b	c	d	o	m	n	p	q	r	k	l	u	v	w	x	y	z	s

The cipher spelling of the word *Patriot* is *revlcqv*.

Tallmadge made four copies of his codebook. He kept one and gave the others to Washington, Woodhull, and Townsend. But even if enemies couldn't break the code, it was dangerous to be caught with anything that looked like a secret message. It was perfect timing for

Dr. James Jay to share his new discovery with General Washington.

Jay was a British doctor who liked to experiment with chemicals. He discovered a way to write an invisible message with one chemical. Then, when he brushed a different chemical over the paper, the message reappeared!

Fortunately, Jay decided to share his secret solutions with the Americans and not the British. It helped that his brother John Jay was a well-known Patriot leader.

Now the Culper spies could send secret messages that no one could see. Even if they were stopped and searched, there was nothing to find.

Washington sent very detailed directions for how the spies should use the ink he called a sympathetic stain: "He should occasionally write his information on the blank leaves of a pamphlet ... or on the blank leaves at each end of registers, almanacs, or any new

publication or book of small value."

Washington also suggested that a good place to hide a secret message would be "between the lines and on the remaining part of a sheet."

● ● ●

Now that the spies knew how to "read between the lines," it was time for the Culper relay to begin. This is how it worked:

First, Townsend (Culper Jr.) gathered intelligence from the British in New York City. He wrote military updates using Tallmadge's cipher codes with invisible ink.

If necessary, Woodhull still made trips to New York. Anna—probably the mystery agent 355 (code for "lady")—may have joined him at times, pretending to be his wife. But usually Roe (agent 724) took the fifty-five-mile trip alone from Setauket to Townsend's store. There he loaded up his wagon with supplies for his tavern. Roe made countless journeys, fooling guards at British checkpoints all along the way.

Under cover of darkness, Roe dropped the spy reports down a hole in one of Woodhull's farm fields. (Spies call this a dead drop.) Once Woodhull uncovered the reports, he added his own intelligence. Then he looked through his spyglass for a signal from Anna's clothesline.

That's right—her clothesline!

When Anna stood on the bluff of Strong's Neck, she could see not only across the Long Island Sound, but also six different coves—three on either side of the point. Brewster gave each cove a number. Once she learned where Brewster was hiding, Anna returned to her clothesline. Then she used her laundry to signal Woodhull across the bay.

When Anna hung a black petticoat on her clothesline, Woodhull knew Brewster was ready for a meeting. The number of handkerchiefs hanging next to the petticoat signaled the cove where he waited. Late at night, Woodhull and Brewster exchanged war secrets in the same tidal marshes they had explored as children.

Brewster was daring but never careless. Hundreds of times, his whaleboat sneaked past British guard boats late at night, carrying secrets across Long Island Sound.

On the Patriot shores of Fairfield, Connecticut,

Tallmadge read the messages. Sometimes he added important information of his own. From there, he or another trusted messenger raced on horseback to deliver the intelligence to General Washington's headquarters in either New Jersey or New York.

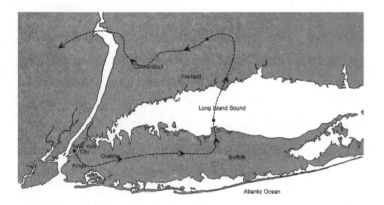

Finally, Washington had a reliable ring of New York spies who could inform him of British activities. There was a lot to report . . . and a lot to fear. Life was dangerous in the British-controlled city and in the towns of Long Island. Enemy troops—and traitors—were everywhere.

Chapter 8

WASHINGTON OUTSMARTS THE BRITISH

Washington relied on the information he received from his Culper spies. He was especially grateful when they tipped him off about a British counterfeiting scheme that would have ruined America's economy and caused the Patriots to lose the war.

But at the same time, the general was frustrated with the lengthy spy relay. Washington wrote to Tallmadge that "the intelligence is so long getting to hand that it is of no use by the time it reaches me."

In the winter of 1780, Washington settled in at his new camp in Morristown, New Jersey. Now that he was stationed northwest of Manhattan, he needed a more direct route for Culper Jr.'s intelligence. It didn't make sense to send messages east to Long Island and then up through Connecticut. Setauket was in the opposite direction from his camp. Much to Woodhull's great disappointment, Washington decided to shut down his faithful Setauket spies.

But only two months later, Washington learned a French fleet was crossing the Atlantic to Rhode Island to join their fight for independence. Support from Britain's rivals was essential to the Americans if they were going to win the war. But did the British know when and where the French would arrive? Washington had to find out in a hurry. He needed Townsend's eyes and ears in New York's seaport.

In July 1780, Washington asked Tallmadge to get the Culper spies back to work—the sooner the better. The Americans' best hope for freedom was on its way. Washington needed to make sure the French troops had a safe landing.

• • •

As soon as Tallmadge received Washington's order to restart the Culper spy ring, the relay began. From Connecticut, Tallmadge passed Washington's request to Brewster, who rowed letters for Culper Jr. and Sr. across the Sound to Setauket. He found Woodhull too ill to travel, so Roe raced to New York City with Washington's urgent letter to Townsend.

Culper Jr. did not delay in gathering the news that his commander needed. He was in the perfect place at the perfect time. As a store owner in the seaport and a Tory reporter, Townsend had every reason to ask about British plans. He had full access to the docks, the bookshops, the taverns, and especially Rivington's coffeehouse—

all the hangouts of the British officers.

It didn't take long for Culper Jr. to get detailed information. He learned how many British ships had arrived and how many troops were shipping out to Newport, Rhode Island, to attack the French. He had to warn Washington!

After Townsend wrote his coded letter for the general, he needed to devise a scheme for Roe to smuggle it past the checkpoints. Since the Redcoats were preparing for an attack, they weren't letting any messengers leave the city. Roe had no trouble *entering* the city to deliver a message to Culper Jr., but how could he sneak a message past British guards on the way out?

Finally, Townsend had an idea: he remembered that Colonel Benjamin Floyd, a Tory from Long Island, had recently been robbed. Townsend wrote a fake letter to Floyd. It stated that Townsend did not have the items that Floyd ordered to replace his stolen goods. Of course,

Floyd had not ordered any goods, but the guards didn't know that.

Roe breezed through each checkpoint with the phony message to Floyd. Between the lines was Townsend's invisible message to Washington, detailing the British plans to attack the French fleet.

Roe, later nicknamed the Paul Revere of Long Island, raced the message back to Setauket in record time. Woodhull added a message to Brewster, also urging a speedy delivery.

When Washington got the news that the British fleet had left New York Harbor and was full speed ahead to Newport, his first thought was to capture New York City. But Washington's commanders assured him that American troops could not hold off a British attack once the royal fleet returned. The Americans needed French troops if they were going to defeat the British. An attack would have to wait.

Instead, George Washington came up with an

ingenious plan. He knew he couldn't outmatch the British, so he would have to outsmart them.

Washington wrote out a fake plot to capture New York. The general's plans detailed an attack on British troops in New York by 12,000 American soldiers—an attack he wished he could really make!

One of Washington's secret agents, pretending to be a Tory farmer, delivered a satchel filled with papers to a British post. He said he found it lying in the road. Perhaps a messenger had dropped it? When Redcoats at the post found battle plans inside—handwritten by General Washington—they must have thought they'd found a treasure. They immediately sent word to the British commander, General Henry Clinton, that the Americans were preparing to capture New York.

General Clinton took the bait. He ordered fires built on Long Island's North Shore to signal the British ships to quickly turn around.

Thanks to Washington's clever trick, the British returned to a peaceful seaport, and the French fleet arrived safely in Newport.

Little did Washington know that while the Culper spies were helping him outsmart the British, one of his most trusted generals was plotting against him.

Chapter 9

TO CATCH A TRAITOR

It's hard to believe that Benedict Arnold, our country's most despised traitor, was once an American war hero. There wasn't a battlefield commander who fought harder for his country. His fearless leadership on the front lines resulted in important victories for the Patriots.

But Arnold had made many enemies. He disobeyed orders when they got in the way of his own plans. Even his brilliant battle victories could not make up for his arrogance. Arnold had few fans in the Continental Congress as well. When they refused to pay him for expenses he couldn't prove, Arnold felt snubbed. A fury grew inside him while he watched others get promotions.

Still, Arnold continued to do what he did best. He charged ahead on the front lines. At the Battle of Saratoga, Arnold proved that he would go to any length to defend his country. He won the battle, but he nearly lost his leg, crushed beneath his fallen horse. His fearlessness paid off and helped turn the tide of the war for the Americans. Finally, Arnold earned praise and a promotion for his heroics.

General Washington considered Arnold one of his most successful commanders. He needed his brilliant leadership on the battlefield. But Arnold's leg was slow to heal. Washington made Arnold the new military governor of Philadelphia to give him more time to recover.

Arnold got off to a shaky start in his new position. He continued to irritate people with his brash behavior and big spending. It didn't help that he spent most of his time with wealthy Loyalists.

Arnold especially enjoyed the company of Peggy Shippen, the beautiful daughter of a Tory judge. He was thrilled when she agreed to marry him. Eager to keep up with his new wife's expensive lifestyle, he sank even deeper into debt.

Benedict Arnold the Patriot couldn't seem to get enough of what he wanted most—money and respect. Perhaps Benedict Arnold the traitor could gain both from the British. They would surely pay him a fortune for Patriot secrets. And if he helped the Redcoats win the war, wouldn't that finally make him a hero?

While Arnold attended parties with his wife in Philadelphia, he secretly made plans to spy for the British. No one knew at the time that Peggy was helping her husband betray his country. But it was no secret she had been a good friend to the British general's closest advisor, Major John André.

Major André was General Clinton's spy

chief—the same position that Major Tallmadge held for General Washington. Unlike Benedict Arnold, John André was a very popular man. He was talented, handsome, and gracious. He charmed Loyalists and Patriots alike with his wit and worldly flair.

Arnold knew that in order to make a deal with Clinton, he would need to go through André. After connecting with him in April 1779, Arnold spent months trying to convince the British spy chief that he would betray the country he had so faithfully defended.

Arnold proved he had no problem spilling Patriot secrets. After all, he was the one who informed the British about the landing of the French fleet in Rhode Island. Fortunately for the Patriots, the Culper spies' fast work kept his betrayal from doing any damage.

Arnold was desperate for money. He demanded to be paid for his secrets. André told

Arnold that General Clinton would make a deal with him once Arnold proved he could help win the war for the British.

Arnold's treasonous plot was already in motion.

• • •

While Benedict Arnold was secretly plotting a betrayal with John André, General Washington was looking for a new commander for the left wing of his army. Washington was disappointed in Arnold's mistakes, but he still considered him his top commander. Washington asked Arnold to take the position. If he had been a loyal Patriot, Arnold would have been honored to accept such a prized post. But his loyalty was already with the enemy.

Arnold claimed his lame leg prevented him from returning to the battlefield. Instead, he convinced Washington to give him command of West Point—the most important military post

in the country. Washington had complete faith in Arnold. The commander of the Continental Army had no idea he was walking into a trap.

The Redcoats were in control of New York City and Long Island in 1780, but the Patriots still controlled the Hudson River. Just north of the city, West Point and its seven forts guarded the Hudson. Sitting high above a bend in the river, the fortress was the perfect lookout for ships sailing between the northern and southern colonies.

As long as the Americans controlled West Point, they controlled the Hudson River. Without it, they would surely lose the war. Benedict Arnold was now in position to make that happen.

Settled in his powerful post at West Point, Arnold finally made his demands. He expected to be paid 20,000 pounds for betraying his country. (That's over three million dollars today.) He also expected a commission as a brigadier general in the British army. In order to seal the deal, Arnold needed to meet with André face to face.

● ● ●

On September 21, 1780, HMS *Vulture,* a British ship, carried André south of West Point for a secret meeting with Arnold. Joshua Smith, a friend of Arnold's who lived close by, escorted the British spy chief to the western shore, where Arnold and André secretly discussed their plan in the woods. At daybreak, they were still plotting, so the spies continued their talks at Smith's house.

The next morning, Arnold took off for

West Point. He needed to return to prepare for Washington's visit. Not only would Arnold hand over West Point to the British, but he hoped to deliver his commander to the enemy as well.

Before he left, Arnold gave André sketches and maps of West Point to deliver to General Clinton. He also wrote a letter for André to carry, allowing him to pass through checkpoints—just in case he was stopped in Patriot territory.

Benedict Arnold knew André's pass might look suspicious. So he wrote letters to Patriot commanders telling them to look out for his secret agent named John Anderson. (That was André's spy name.) Arnold even wrote a letter to Tallmadge, asking that if he met Anderson, he should deliver him to Arnold.

Tallmadge had never been a fan of Arnold's. They had both lived in New Haven when Tallmadge attended Yale. Tallmadge recalled having "the belief that he was not a man of integrity." He thought Arnold's request was very strange. Why would the commander of West Point need his own spy?

Smith waited until dark to take André to the boat that would ferry him back to HMS *Vulture*. Just as Smith and André were leaving the house, they heard a loud explosion. Patriot cannonballs were firing on the British ship. The captain had no choice but to leave André behind!

André would have to travel by land instead. He put on civilian clothes and headed with Smith toward the British checkpoint at White Plains. Soon after Smith left André, who continued on his own, three Patriot militiamen stopped the spy. Unfortunately for André, he thought they were Loyalists. He told them he was a British officer.

The militiamen acted more like robbers than soldiers. They were willing to let the captured Redcoat go if they could have his money, his horse, his watch—and his boots.

But when they took his boots, they found André's hidden spy papers. So they decided to take his things *and* turn him in. Arnold's pass did him no good at all. The soldiers delivered André to the closest Patriot post.

Colonel John Jameson, the commander in charge, was shocked when they brought in their prisoner. Jameson had received one of General Arnold's letters saying to look out for a Mr. John Anderson, who might be traveling in Patriot territory. But here was a British officer with the same name carrying treasonous letters written by Benedict Arnold!

The colonel didn't know what to do. But he knew he didn't want to anger Arnold. So Jameson decided to send the prisoner to West Point with a note for Arnold. It explained that the British officer was found with papers of "a very dangerous tendency," which Jameson was sending to General Washington.

It just so happened that Tallmadge arrived at Jameson's post at the time of André's capture. The spy chief remembered Arnold's strange message and insisted he take charge of the prisoner himself.

There was no doubt in Tallmadge's mind that General Arnold was a traitor. He wanted to send troops to arrest him for treason, but Jameson refused, worrying Arnold might have an explanation for the strange circumstances. What if Tallmadge was wrong? Finally, Jameson agreed to let Tallmadge take André with him. But he insisted on sending the note of explanation to Benedict Arnold.

Once André was told his secret papers about West Point were being sent to Washington, he knew he was trapped. André asked to write a letter of confession to General Washington. He admitted he was not John Anderson, a Patriot secret agent, but Major John André, General Clinton's chief of intelligence.

Tallmadge guessed that as soon as Arnold received Jameson's message, he would send British troops to rescue André in White Plains. So Tallmadge decided to move André to another Patriot base.

It was a revealing journey for the two spy chiefs. Tallmadge found André to be as likable as any man he had ever met. Just like Nathan Hale, he was loyally serving his country. And just like Hale, he was headed for hanging.

But unlike the young Patriot volunteer, André was an adjutant general to the British commander. Washington hoped André's high rank and outstanding reputation would ensure his exchange for Benedict Arnold, his most valued commander, who nearly won the war for England. But General Clinton would not give up Arnold.

John André faced his death with the same

grace and courage he showed in life. His last words were: "I pray you bear me witness that I met my fate like a brave man." Tallmadge, there to witness André's terrible fate—the same as his dear friend Nathan Hale's—was brought to tears. He wrote, "I cannot say enough of his fortitude—unfortunate youth; I wish Arnold had been in his place."

André would become a beloved hero in Britain, just as Nathan Hale would become in America.

While André faced his destiny with honor, Arnold acted the coward. An hour before Washington was due to arrive, Arnold received Jameson's message that André and the maps of West Point had been captured. After saying good-bye to Peggy, Arnold secretly raced off to his private boat. While his oarsmen rowed him to British protection on HMS *Vulture,* Peggy pretended to be shocked by the news of her husband's betrayal and escape. It would be many years before Americans learned that she had been a partner to his treason all along.

Because of Jameson's interference, Benedict Arnold slipped from the grasp of the Patriots. Yet due to Tallmadge's quick thinking, Washington, West Point, and the Continental army were saved from almost certain defeat.

Chapter 10

A SPY HUNT
AND A VICTORY

Unfortunately, before Tallmadge knew Arnold's true motives, he had shared dangerous secrets with the traitor. He had written Arnold about British intelligence he had received from a trusted secret agent in New York City. Fortunately, he did not reveal Culper Jr.'s code name or identity. But now Arnold knew Washington had New York spies—and he was desperate to find them.

Arnold already knew Brewster smuggled messages back and forth across Long Island Sound. He also knew that Colonel Simcoe had accused Woodhull of being a spy, although the British had no proof.

The British couldn't trace Townsend, Roe, Woodhull, or the "certain woman," as they referred to Anna Smith Strong. Still, the Culper spies knew they were in grave danger. They heard reports of Patriot spies being captured—and killed—in Arnold's ruthless hunts. And now he was hunting for them!

All Culper spy communications stopped. Tallmadge reported to Washington that it was too risky for his spies to gather and send intelligence.

Fortunately, Washington's New York spy ring was able to dodge Arnold. And while they stayed out of harm's way, the most unlikely link to the Culper Spy Ring was making a move that would help defeat the British, once and for all.

● ● ●

As it turned out, Robert Townsend wasn't the only reporter gathering British secrets for

Washington. James Rivington, the publisher of the *Royal Gazette,* who was named the Printer to the King's Most Excellent Majesty, also spied for General Washington! The most hated Tory in New York was the last person anyone would suspect as a Patriot spy. He regularly printed abusive and untrue stories about George Washington. His coffeehouse was a favorite hangout for British officers. John André was a frequent guest and even had his love poems printed in the *Royal Gazette.*

Washington had instructed the Culper spies to write their invisible messages inside books and journals—many of which came from Rivington's bookstore. After the war, it was discovered that Rivington often added secret messages of his own to Washington in Roe's deliveries. When Tallmadge's codebook was revealed, Rivington's name was listed along with the other Culper spies. His code number was 726.

Although many of the details of his assistance

may never be uncovered, there is little doubt that Rivington helped win the war for America.

Somehow the Loyalist publisher got his hands on the secret codebook for the flags that signaled orders between British ships. He smuggled it to the French commander Admiral François-Joseph-Paul de Grasse in time for the French fleet to block nineteen British warships from entering the Chesapeake Bay. General Charles Cornwallis, the British southern commander, couldn't organize a British defense in Yorktown, Virginia, without the northern troops.

Thanks to the codebook that Rivington stole, they never got there!

On September 28, 1781, 17,000 American and French troops surrounded Cornwallis's 8,000 troops in Yorktown. There was no way the Redcoats in the north could get to Yorktown to join the fight. And there was no way Cornwallis's troops could get out.

After two weeks, Cornwallis surrendered. The Continental army had done the impossible—they had outsmarted the Redcoats and had earned their independence from Britain.

Chapter 11

TILL DEATH
DO US PART

It would take two more years before America and Britain would sign a peace treaty in Paris. Loyalists were no longer welcome in New York. Thousands of Tories packed up and moved to England. Thousands of others started new lives in Canada.

Washington's Culper spies didn't breathe a word of their heroic contributions to winning the war. They had not risked their lives for praise. They had not spied for money. Most of them took their secrets to their graves. While America celebrated its independence, the Culper spies quietly returned to their lives.

There would be no parades, no memorials, and no holidays in honor of these American heroes. They didn't need anyone else to know how they helped George Washington outsmart the British. It was much easier—and safer—for them to keep their adventures to themselves.

In November 1783, General Washington led his Continental Army in a victory tour through the streets of New York City. While he was there, he made only a few stops. The first shocked everyone. The commander in chief paid a visit to James Rivington! No one could believe the general was paying his respects to the hated Loyalist who repeatedly published insulting articles and cartoons about the commander and his troops.

Finally, the world would learn that Rivington had been a secret agent for America. No doubt, Washington hoped his public thank-you would ensure his safety.

• • •

Seven years later, in 1790, President George Washington took a horse-drawn carriage tour of Long Island. He returned to thank the Long Island Patriots—and, most likely, his Culper spies—for their loyal service during the war. President Washington wrote in his diary that he spent the night at Austin Roe's tavern during that trip. If Washington met and thanked his Setauket spies that day, he kept it a secret.

It seems impossible to think that Washington's only spy ring could keep their heroic adventures from the world—and, in some cases, even from their own families. But then again, they were masters at keeping secrets.

THE RING IS COMPLETE

Just as they had agreed, George Washington never met Townsend during the war—nor did they ever meet later. Washington would never even learn Culper Jr.'s real name.

It wasn't until 1939 that Morton Pennypacker, a Long Island historian, discovered Culper Jr.'s true identity. Pennypacker had studied the historic letters between Washington and his New York spies. He knew their handwriting as well as his own.

When the Townsend family papers from Oyster Bay were given to him, he noticed something familiar about Robert Townsend's handwriting. Even the paper used looked familiar.

Pennypacker had a thought: Could Townsend, the aloof and studious merchant, be the same daring agent who fed Washington some of the most important secrets of the Revolutionary War? Pennypacker compared Townsend's papers to Culper Jr.'s spy letters. A handwriting expert proved his hunch was correct.

More than 150 years after the end of the Revolutionary War, the mystery of the key Culper spy in Washington's historic spy ring was solved.

Finally, the ring was complete once again.

THE STORY BEHIND THE STORY

GEORGE WASHINGTON'S SPIES

Ever since he was a boy, George Washington had dreamed of following in his older half brother's footsteps. Lawrence Washington was raised more like an Englishman than a Virginia colonist. He attended school in England and bravely served as a captain under British Vice Admiral Edward Vernon. (Lawrence's plantation, Mount Vernon—which George inherited—was named after Edward Vernon.) After returning to Virginia, Lawrence became a

Mount Vernon

successful and respected land-owner and businessman.

Fourteen years younger than Lawrence, George was only eleven when their father died. George did not go to England for a gentleman's education, staying in Virginia with his mother. Three years later, Lawrence arranged for George to join the Royal Navy as a midshipman, but with advice from her brother, George's mother forbade it. Lawrence guided George on a different path to becoming a colonial

gentleman. Surveying land helped George increase his own wealth, but he still dreamed of a British military commission.

When George was twenty years old, Lawrence died from tuberculosis. All at once, George lost his brother, his best friend, and his role model. But even after his death, Lawrence still guided his younger brother's future. Lawrence's vacant post in Virginia's colonial militia gave George the opportunity he needed. Major Washington— finally a soldier—was determined to honor his brother and make his country proud.

USE TALLMADGE'S NUMERICAL DICTIONARY TO DECIPHER THESE MESSAGES:

First Message:
723. knows of 178.592.

Second Message:
724. will 156.356. to 722. in 729.

Third Message:
725. will 156.174.356. of great 317. to 721.,
who will 156. to 711. at 727.73.

If you'd like to see samples of Tallmadge's original Culper Code
Book, visit mountvernon.org.

ODE	MEANING
711	General Washington
712	General Clinton
713	Governor Tryon
721	Major Tallmadge (alias John Bolton)
722	Abraham Woodhull (alias Culper Sr.)
723	Robert Townsend (alias Culper Jr.)
724	Austin Roe
725	Caleb Brewster
726	James Rivington
727	New York
728	Long Island
729	Setauket
745	England

CODE	MEANING
15	advice
28	appointment
48	be
60	better
73	camp
87	careful
121	day
156	deliver
178	enemy
174	express
317	importance
356	letter
371	man
476	parts
585	refugees
592	ships
660	vigilant
680	war
691	written

ANSWERS:

1. Culper Jr. knows of enemy ships.

2. Austin Roe will deliver letter to Culper Sr. in Setauket.

3. Caleb Brewster will deliver express letter of great importance to John Bolton, who will deliver to General Washington at New York camp.

THEIR STORIES AFTER THE WAR

Benjamin Tallmadge, agent 721, lived in Litchfield, Connecticut, until his death at the age of eighty-one. Within a year after the war, Tallmadge married Mary Floyd. She was related to Colonel Benjamin Floyd—the Tory who was the pretend recipient of some of Townsend's spy letters! Tallmadge served eight terms in Congress and made his fortune from the Ohio Company—a western expansion group that Lawrence Washington and Governor Dinwiddie had invested in before the French and Indian War. Later in life, Tallmadge's children urged him to write down his experiences in the Revolutionary War. In his memoir, published in 1858, this is all he had to say about his role as spymaster of the first and most successful spy ring in American history:

This year [1778] I opened a private correspondence with some persons in New York (for Gen. Washington) which lasted through the war. How beneficial it was to the Commander-in-Chief is evidenced by his continuing the same to the close of the war. I kept one or more boats continually employed in crossing the Sound on this business.

Abraham Woodhull, agent 722, married Mary Smith in 1781. Two of their three children married Brewsters. Woodhull was a respected judge and lived to be seventy-six years old without anyone knowing his secret identity as Culper Sr.

Caleb Brewster, agent 725, married Anne Lewis the year after the war ended. They raised eight children on their farm in Fairfield, Connecticut. Brewster was a blacksmith and a member of the US Revenue Cutter Service, now known as the Coast Guard. He lived to be eighty years old.

Once the British left Setauket, Selah Strong finally returned to his devoted wife, **Anna Smith Strong**, who may have been agent 355. Soon after the war ended, Anna and Selah had their ninth and last child, George Washington Strong. They enjoyed a long and peaceful life together at their family estate on Strong's Neck in Setauket.

Austin Roe, courier agent 724, was the only Culper spy other than Anna Smith Strong who had been married during the war. He and his wife continued to run their tavern and inn after the war. Roe had eight children and lived to be eighty-one years old.

Robert Townsend, agent 723, was the only Culper spy who never married. He lived with his sister, Sally, at their family home in Oyster Bay, where he remained sullen for the rest of his life. Some say he became bitter because he was never rewarded for his loyal service and sacrifices. Others think the stress from the perils of war was too great for him to overcome. While Townsend may not have lived as happily as his Culper partners after the war, he did live a long life, dying at the age of eighty-four.

James Rivington, agent 726, was given Patriot protection at the end of the war while other Loyalists were forced from America. Even though Washington paid a public visit to Rivington at his bookshop, Sons of Liberty members continued to torment the Tory publisher for the rest of his life. Rivington was forced to shut down his printing press on December 31, 1783. He remained a bookseller in New York City but never met with success again and ended up in debtors' prison. About a year after he was released, Washington's most surprising spy died on July 4, 1802, at the age of seventy-eight.

After betraying the country he had so bravely served, **Benedict Arnold** had hoped for a hero's welcome from the British. But even as a Redcoat, Arnold was disliked and distrusted for the rest of his life. His military and business ventures in England, Canada, and the West Indies were all failures. Benedict Arnold died in London, poor and forgotten. He and his loyal wife, Peggy, had five children. She paid off her husband's debts after his death and died three years later.

How do you honor one of the greatest Revolutionary war heroes when he is also America's most despised traitor? John Watts de Peyster, a Civil War major general, found a way. Without a face or name to accompany it, De Peyster donated a monument of a boot to recognize Benedict Arnold's leg injuries at the Battle of Saratoga, which ended his battlefield career. His heroic victory was considered the turning point of the war for the Patriots.

Benedict Arnold's Boot Monument
Saratoga National Historical Park, New York

For Further Reading

Allen, Thomas B. *George Washington, Spymaster: How America Outspied the British and Won the Revolutionary War.* Washington, D.C.: National Geographic, 2004.

Bliven, Bruce, Jr. *The American Revolution.* New York: Random House, 1981.

Edwards, Roberta. *Who Was George Washington?* New York: Grosset & Dunlap, 2009.

Fritz, Jean. *Traitor: The Case of Benedict Arnold.* Unforgettable Americans. New York: Puffin, 1997.

Hale, Nathan*. *Nathan Hale's Hazardous Tales: One Dead Spy.* New York: Amulet/Abrams, 2012.

Heilbroner, Joan. *Meet George Washington.* Landmark Books. New York: Random House, 2001.

*Not the same Nathan Hale this book is about!

Recommended Websites

For more information about George Washington:

mountvernon.org

For more about the Culper Spy Ring and Revolutionary War espionage:

mountvernon.org/george-washington/
the-revolutionary-war/spying-and-espionage

For primary source material about George Washington and the Culper Spy Ring:

guides.library.stonybrook.edu
/c.php?g=35445&p=225141

New friends. New adventures.
Find a new series ... just for yo

BALLPARK *Mysteries*

FOR THE SPORTS FAN

THE DINO FILES

FOR THE ADVENTURER

Louise Trapeze

FOR THE SUPERSTAR

PIPER GREEN

FOR THE DREAMER

PUPPY PIRATES

FOR THE ANIMAL LOVER

Totally True adventures!

FOR THE EXPLORER

RandomHouseKids.com